Love Me or Go to Hell

Other Books by Donna Barstow

What Do Women Really Want? Chocolate!

To Connie –

Love Me or Go to Hell

TRUE LOVE CARTOONS

Who was as boycrazy as me!!

Donna L. Barstow
Editor and Cartoonist

Love
Donna
xx oo

Cartoons also by:

Liza Donnelly   Stephanie Piro
Anne Gibbons   Lynn Williams

**Andrews McMeel
Publishing**

Kansas City

Love Me or Go to Hell

06 07 08 09 BID 10 9 8 7 6 5 4 3 2

ISBN-13: 978-0-7407-5698-6
ISBN-10: 0-7407-5698-2

Library of Congress Control Number: 2005931404

www.andrewsmcmeel.com

ATTENTION: SCHOOLS AND BUSINESSES
Andrews McMeel books are available at quantity discounts with bulk purchase for educational, business, or sales promotional use. For information, please write to: Special Sales Department, Andrews McMeel Publishing, 4520 Main Street, Kansas City, Missouri 64111.

To Dad

and

to every bird I've ever known

Foreword

I love men. I love being in a relationship with a man. I love the feeling of being in love. You probably do, too. But if we're honest with ourselves as women, we must confess the whole truth: *Men can drive us completely crazy.* They can transform us from centered and independent into needy and insecure with just one look or remark. They can turn us from calm and serene beings into exasperated, raving maniacs. And let's face it—no matter how smart we believe we are in other areas of our life, when it comes to love, we've all had our *"I can't believe I did that/felt that/dated him/fell for that"* moments.

These are confessions that only another woman can truly make or understand. But before you blame yourself for your less-than-perfect love life, remember that no part of having a relationship is easy. It's difficult to find the right partner, to get along with him, and to keep the magic and passion alive year after year. We do our best, always trying to improve ourselves (and our mates, of course!). Yet there are moments when it helps to know that we're not the only one trying to stay afloat as we bob up and down on the often turbulent sea of love.

One of the most precious things in the world is a caring and compassionate girlfriend who listens to you, gets what you're saying immediately, and helps you lighten up—just when you need it the most. That's how I see this delightful book. It is like the best friend who can make you smile, giggle, and feel better about whatever situation you are in. It is like the clever friend who can find humor even in what seems to be the most depressing circumstances. And it is like the most compassionate friend who can always make you laugh—even at yourself!

As you experience the cartoons on these pages, you will find yourself nodding enthusiastically, sighing with empathy, and chuckling with recognition at the situations and emotions captured so perfectly in the words and drawings. Hopefully, in the midst of these thoughts, you will also have a wonderful realization: *It's not just you! You're not alone. We're all in this together.*

Enjoy, and remember not to be so hard on yourself. Love's a crazy thing.

BARBARA DE ANGELIS
Barbara De Angelis is the author of fourteen best—selling books on love, relationships, and personal growth. Learn more at www.BarbaraDeAngelis.com.

SHARON LIKED TO SCREEN
MEN BEFORE A DATE.

D. Barstow

"You're in shoe sales? Say no more. I'm yours!"

"I get the feeling you're one of those *Sex and the City* type women, Dina . . . which, personally, I find a little scary!"

"I wish we lived in a simpler time . . . when all we had to do was heave our bosoms to get a man's attention!"

"I'm already booked for a spring fling.
Can I pencil you in for a summer tryst?"

"Who knows, maybe we'll meet great guys this time."

"Maybe we should just go back to e-mailing . . ."

"Don't look now, but here comes a cutie pie. He could be a puppet, a pirate, a poet, a pauper . . . or a prince!"

"Thanks, Eric, but I'm not wearing any.
You're smelling my latest magazines."

LINDA TRIED TO KEEP AN OPEN MIND
ABOUT HER BLIND DATE.

D. Barstow

"I'm calling you to tell you I'm *not* calling you . . .
because I'm the girl! And, by the way,
who makes up these stupid rules, anyway?"

"Plenty of men have made me cry. It's nice to finally
meet a man who can make me laugh!"

"You know, Dennis, I've never been good with figures.
Stick figures, I mean."

"I believe we have something in common.
I, too, love chocolate ice cream."

D. Barstow

"I do date geeks from time to time,
but the training period is brutal."

"The parking attendant sent it over,
with warm regards."

An easy way to tell
the boys from the men.

D. Barstow

"We met in a recovery program,
with separate, yet compatible, addictions."

"You're much too gorgeous to be serious about, Byron, but let me enjoy the moment!"

"I always practice catch and release.
When I'm feeling kindhearted, that is . . ."

"You're not a fixer-upper, are you?
I'm looking for someone in move-in condition."

"Hello, I'm Kevin, and I'll be your lover tonight."

"It's harder to meet men in the fall and winter . . .
they return to their lairs till spring!"

"I met Carl on this Renaissance Web site, where he's lord of a small kingdom. He's quite the catch!"

"Uh, Michael, my ad said I want a man who is *serious*, not *curious*."

"I picked him up here a couple of nights ago, but he's the wrong size. Do you accept returns or refunds?"

"Don't wait up. When you're dating one of the
undead you keep ungodly hours!"

"But what if he *is* the perfect man?"

"Ask him what he does. And how long he does it."

"I've gone *there* for lots of dates."

"Well, Margaret W., did you follow *The Rules*? There's a good reason that book was written, you know!"

"Have you had your downtown shots?
'Cause you're going to be exposed to
massive amounts of art, culture, and cool guys!"

"I don't plan to marry.
I'll just have to be a Desperate Girlfriend."

"There goes Trent . . . just looking at him causes scars!"

"Three little words to keep in mind, missy.
Cow. Milk. Free."

"I'm in love with Ted! I've got the heart that cried wolf . . . but I'm going to trust it one more time!"

"I like to date younger men once in a while.
It makes me feel naughty and daring . . .
like sneaking a chocolate bar on your diet!"

"This is a commitment shirt! My boyfriend left it at my place. That means he's coming back!"

"I guess you could say we're getting serious . . .
we went to look at condoms yesterday."

"It's the usual stuff. He's yin, I'm yang.
And feng shui didn't help."

Lynn Williams

"We met in a chat room. I know his dark side,
but I still don't know his last name."

"I was just discussing intimacy issues with my boyfriend, and he spontaneously combusted! I should have known better."

"We forget, sometimes, that men are people, too. They have feelings. At least, some of them seem to. Well, I think George does, anyhow!"

"Here's my flower garden . . . roses, lilies, daisies . . .
It's called, optimistically, bridal bouquet mix!"

"You know what to do, Jennifer—back up, back up, back up. Even if you didn't meet him online."

"When Tom left, I took up knitting. I don't knit anything in particular . . . just the physical expression of my pain, in wool, which can be worn as a scarf."

"What can I tell you? He's cute, sweet, and intelligent—sort of the pick of the single, available male litter!"

"So tell me. Who did you do on
your summer vacation?"

"I'm not ready to find the right man yet. I want a few years of messing with the wrong ones first!"

"He makes me so mad, I could tear my hair out!
Uh, forget that. I could muss it up really badly!"

"I don't knit, but do you mind if I just hang out and bitch? It's my ex-boyfriends, see . . ."

"Ahhh, sweet, salty, sour, bitter.
Just like the four stages of my last relationship."

"Wear pink. Make him think you're
softer than you really are."

"I'm dating a guy I *know* is all wrong for me.
I bought a ticket on the train wreck called love!"

"Club Med. I went, I loved, I conquered!"

"I *said* he's *okay*, Marsha, he just doesn't
seem like the *beach* type to me."

"Here, try my SPF 35:
Waterproof, sweatproof, and jerkproof."

"I don't know if he's spongeworthy yet,
but I do heart him!"

"Like my mother always says, it's as easy to
fall in love with an office drone
as it is with a blue-collar worker."

"Helpless, perhaps, but not hopeless.
Your turn or mine?"

"Did I tell you about David? He fit perfectly in between my kicky fall suede booties and my spring peekaboo Jimmy Choo shoes."

After my breakup, a younger man has refreshed my palette for men again...
Boy sorbet?
D. Barstow

"I suppose men aren't too different from women . . .
women who've been abducted by aliens!"

"Here are my last three men,
and here are our last meals."

"I wouldn't say I'm his most successful relationship . . .
I'd say I've stayed on the bull the longest!"

"What's different?
Have you had a boyfriend enhancement?"

"How do you and Joe divvy up household chores?
So far, I'm just making Harry do everything."

"Or you could find out right *now* if he's a Bad Boy . . .
Just throw him in the pool, and see if he floats or sinks!"

"My new boss is rather studly . . .
in a gold chains kind of way!"

"For Jim's birthday I'm giving him boxer shorts with pink flowers all over them. A present for *both* of us!"

"There's nothing like an old-fashioned love letter
to make us both feel like we've won the lottery."

"Diane, you're such a workaholic! Take the afternoon off, and let's go whistle at construction workers!"

D. Barstow

"I thought about getting my teeth whitened,
but I don't want to look predatory."

"Jeffrey's taken up golf. It's opened up a whole new world of things to fight about."

"We've worked out a compromise. I go to the games with him, but I don't have to eat a hot dog."

"I guess I'm confused. I sent him a Dear John letter, but I put a love stamp on it."

"I've always been attracted to alpha males, because they know how to appreciate alpha females like me!"

"I hate to admit it, but my self-esteem is directly related to the number of calls on my answering machine, cell phone, and beeper. And geeks don't count."

DIVA POSE #1.
IT'S ALL ABOUT ME

DIVA POSE #2.
SALUTATION OF THE BLING-BLING

"Nothing like a bath to wash away all life's troubles . . .
oh, you're still here?"

"My problem is that I love too big . . . it scares guys off.
I need to go on an emotional diet!"

"Until I find my one true love,
MAC is my makeup boyfriend."

"I threw Steve out the window the other day.
It's about taking care of _me._"

"What age is our zenith? I don't want to waste
it on the wrong relationship . . ."

"He looked like my father and sounded like my mother.
Was that so wrong?"

"I'll have the linguini in commitment sauce."

"Uh–oh, catastrophic meteorite headed this way . . . but on the plus side, your love life will really pick up!"

"A man can only satisfy a woman's needs just so far . . .
for the rest, there's dark chocolate truffles.
One pound, please. And hurry!"

"Hello, do you have a perfume that suggests
'Sex Goddess,' with an undernote that says,
'But I'm really really picky'?"

"Women think about a lot more than just clothes
and relationships . . . We're plotting to take over the
world, too, or didn't you know?"

"It's very sweet of you, Rick,
but I've fallen in love with myself again."

"My beauty regime consists of eating right, exercise, and at least eight hours' sleep with a good-looking man!"

"It's the time of month when I crave chocolate.
Get away! I crave *that* two weeks from now!"

"Then he asked me if *his* jeans made *him* look fat. So I said, 'Whoa, buddy! There's only room for one narcissist in here.'"

"I just wasn't that into him."

"This could be the start of something stupid."

"I don't mean to treat you like a sex object . . .
all those issues of *Cosmo* have gone to my head!"

"You must be Kenny. Jill's still sharpening her nails."

"In a world of cheap screwtops, you are definitely
my special private reserve."

"Consider me your own personal homeland security!
I'll walk you home and stay all night, if you'd like!"

"I think the *Kama Sutra* forgot hot cocoa kisses."

"It must have been a good night."

"Ooh, flowers! Come here, you!
Time for some positive reinforcement!"

D. Barstow

"Can you recommend a wine to celebrate both a promotion and something new going on in the bedroom?"

"You want me to do what?
Sorry to disillusion you . . . but you really have high
expectations in the romance department!"

"I love the way you brood. Very sexy!"

"You're still the sexiest man I know! Of course,
I work at home, alone, and you're the only guy I see.
But we'll give you the benefit of the doubt!"

"I'm sorry, Nick, but you can't have *all* of my attention *all* of the time."

"Sorry for interrupting, darling, but I just find a man
doing a crossword puzzle sooo sexy!"

"Before you kiss me goodnight, let me offer you a choice of lip glosses . . . mint, cherry, or beer!"

"I should tell you up front, John,
I've never been good at hiding my feelings."

"Are you surprised? I've got a very passionate nature.
It doesn't always come across at work!"

"How do you feel about a kissing tutorial?
After all, this is the Show–Me state . . ."

"There are *some* things a woman can fake, Liam,
but being in love isn't one of them!"

"The girl you asked out at the office becomes the surprising woman you didn't expect at home!"

"Harold, I've never been brave enough to tell you I love you, so tonight . . . I'm letting the merlot speak for me!"

"When did business turn so dramatically to pleasure?"

"Sorry, Kevin, it turns out Spike *did* like you, but we both think you smell like a man with a small income."

Lynn Williams

"It was a fair settlement. He got the wide-screen TV,
and I got the cats and the vet."

"We have *so* much in common! Now, tell me . . .
how do you feel about cats?"

"He's allowed to ignore me . . . he's a cat. You're not!"

"Oh, sure! Go right ahead! Side with him against me!"

"I can't make any promises, Brad, but you might consider getting a little work done on your beak."

"We all love you anyway,
not just because you give off the most heat!"

"The cat only loves you best because you feed her.
Come to think of it . . . I love you best, too!"

"Well, I'm sorry, too, Myrna, but nobody *made* you eat him afterward."

"Relax! You'll forget they're there after a while!"

"Just a martini and crackers? You're beautiful,
but kooky, you know that?"

"This is *World of Animals*. Scientists know now why men jump off cliffs into the ocean: fear of commitment. But what about lemmings? What's *their* problem?"

"It could never work out, Bruce.
You're a cat person and I'm a dog person."

"If we had kids, do you think they'd look like me . . .
or you? It should be me, since the
dog resembles you already!"

"Trevor found my G spot! Third finger, left hand!"

"I will love you and honor your screenplays for as
long as we both shall live."

"If Anne Rice and Stephen King ever fell in love and got married, that'd *almost* be as cool as you and me!"

"Of course I'll marry you!
There's no one I'd rather be in debt with!"

"I love you, too, Edward. But I think we both know that true love begins only after shelling out three months' salary on a quality diamond ring . . ."

"And do you, Lisa, take Bill, including his issues,
to love and deal with, as long as you both shall live?"

"Do you promise to love, honor, and cherish her,
and never tell her she looks fat?
Even on those 'special' days?"

"Big ring, big you-know-what,
that's been my experience."

"I think love is contagious! I caught it from you!"

"I always wanted a man to put me on a pedestal!
Thanks! I kind of like it up here!"

"I'd like a chardonnay,
and I'm fairly certain he'd like sex."

DONNELLY

"You don't say much . . . that's what I like about you.
I get ample airtime."

"You're turning off emotionally! I can tell!
The red light's gone out!"

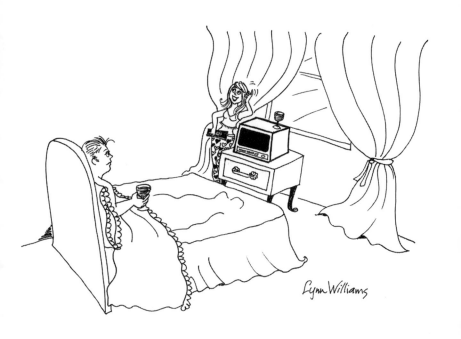

"What luck! Tonight's the premiere of the 'Him Improvement Network.'"

"Not tonight, Monique. I'm feeling wimpy."

"It says here Americans work the way the French make love. Are we living in the wrong country or what?"

Lynn Williams

"Well, so much for our hot summer romance."

"I'm past the stage where looking at you is enough!
Next time we eat out, you take the 'wall' seat!"

"Love means I'm always right!
You didn't read the fine print on our wedding vows!"

"Hey! You never noticed my new shoes! Pay attention!"

"He has your number, but he'll never call you.
And he slept with your best friend."

"Tom, I'm beginning to think you buy me flowers
so you can hide behind them . . . Tom?"

"You might be the one for me. I won't be sure till I
do some further studies in the field."

"A penny for your thoughts."

"We've been much happier since we broke up."

"I said I love you . . . now, you're supposed to say it back! You'll get the hang of this if it kills me!"

Lynn Williams

"Did I say milquetoast?
I meant milk chocolate. Go get me some."

"You know, Charles, I'm liking this raw side of you."

"So you feel comfortable with the fact that
my genes are dominant, and yours are recessive?"

"A man who can dance
wins my heart every time!"

When Ellen saw her insanely jealous ex-boyfriend
heading up the aisle at the end of the movie,
she knew she had to act quickly.

"Oh, look, the big bad storm cloud is passing over . . . and right behind it, here comes the rainbow of love!"

"It's a minimalist tree, darling. But the presents should be maximum . . . for balance!"

"Now that we're serious, I think I can wean you off the personality that was trying to impress you with a clean apartment!"

"Isn't it great, being in love? It's like a new hobby we both have in common!"

"Nothing special.
Just celebrating your coming home from work!"

"We both look so *hot* tonight, people must be
wondering which of us is the arm candy!"

"When I'm around you, I can't think straight!
What do you call that? Love?"

"Darling, the only thing I don't have
to redecorate is you!"

"He costs just pennies a day to operate."

DONNELLY

"Maybe we'll be together again in another life.
Or when you get a job."

"Actually, I like the Vandycke now.
It's the rest of you I don't like."

"Help me with this, Michael.
Something's bothering you, isn't it?"

"Tom, can't you see that she's just *using* you?"

"Yes, I do like you, Jim, but that's not why
I called this meeting."

"You want to break up with me because I'm too vain?
How can you say such a thing!"

"How do I love thee? Let me count
the ways and wherefores."

"I couldn't find the deductible line
for my loser boyfriend."

"We make a good team, because my attributes overpower your defects. Oh, and vice versa, of course . . ."

"I don't want to see you anymore, Gary. I just hate it
when men try to sell you T-shirts afterward."

"You never write me poetry any more. And when you *do*, it's bad poetry."

"You know how I feel about commercialized holidays,
but I'll be your anti–valentine, if you'd like!"

"I never noticed how boring you are
when you watch TV."

"My love for you is a big, heart-shaped feeling inside,
filled with springtime and moonlight!
Now, describe your love for me!"

"He's the lemon in my hot fudge sundae."

"Oh, look! Love is in the air!"